1995

Celebrating School Liturgies: Guidelines for Planning

Written by Joan Patano Vos
Edited by Timothy J. Vos

THE LITURGICAL PRESS
Collegeville, Minnesota

Cover design by David Manahan, O.S.B.

1   2   3   4   5   6   7   8   9

Library of Congress Cataloging-in-Publication Data

Vos, Joan Patano, 1955-
    Celebrating school liturgies : guidelines for planning / written by Joan Patano Vos ; edited by Timothy J. Vos.
        p. cm.
    ISBN 0-8146-1906-1
    1. Liturgy committees—Catholic Church. 2. Catholic schools--United States. 3. Worship (Religious education) 4. Catholic Church—Liturgy. 5. Catholic Church—Education—United States. I. Vos, Timothy J., 1954- . II. Title.
    BX1970.5.V67   1991
    264'.02—dc20   90-27537
                                                                   CIP

Acknowledgements———————

This booklet was first conceived as a teaching aid in consultation with representatives of the Wichita Catholic Schools in 1987. Our thanks go to Kathy Faulkner, Ladene Herrick, Ann Johnson, Nell Kaba, and Diana Knolla. Their ideas provided impetus for the work.

We also wish to thank Bishop Eugene Gerber and the people of the diocese of Wichita, who welcomed and supported us in our work throughout their community.

Contents

"Liturgy is the work of the people."

Introduction

This book is a tool for adults who are endeavoring to help students pray liturgically. At the heart of the book lies one simple form—*The Basics* form (p. 23)—that guides teachers through the essential steps of preparing themselves and students for liturgy and then planning that liturgy with the students.

The text of the book is organized in three sections:

"The Basics" offers valuable insights and expands our understanding of the essential elements of liturgy.

"Beyond the Basics" offers suggestions and ideas for more extensive liturgical preparation and planning, if time and resources permit.

"The Liturgy of the Hours" provides teachers and students with an explanation of Morning and Evening Prayer for daytime or evening classroom use.

Each of these sections, organized around topical headings, is accompanied by simple forms that incorporate the essentials of that section. Use of these forms can streamline preparation and planning for liturgy and can facilitate communication among students, teachers, and presiders.

Just as faith is transmitted by people and not by curriculum, so, too, we learn how to pray—and how to pray liturgically—through the love and example of others. In preparing for liturgy, we leave the *love* up to you! And we offer some suggestions for providing students with an informed example of how we can approach developing good liturgy. It is our hope that teachers as well as students will come to a greater practical knowledge and a deeper understanding of liturgical prayer through the use of this book.

We begin by introducing some basic questions. What is liturgy? What is liturgical prayer?

The word "liturgy" comes from a Greek word that means "the work of the people." Liturgy is a communal act of worship in which we use symbols and symbolic language. These symbols operate on two different levels—the level of expression and the level of formation. We express what we are about as a people of God, and in doing so we are further formed into that people of God.

Prayer is our turning to God, our remembering God in all that we do. To pray liturgically means to pray with ritual and symbol, as community. At liturgical prayer we practice the act of surrendering our own will to that of our Creator. In the process we are united as a people of God, whose purpose it is to transform the earthly world into a new creation under the reign of God. Thus, what we do at liturgy is far bigger than who we are as individuals. We gather, as individuals, to be formed into a community bound by a covenant of love to our Creator.

THREE BASIC THOUGHTS

Here are some fundamentals to keep in mind when preparing for liturgy. We hope they might help to focus new understandings:

Prayer happens not just with words. Prayer happens—or is formed—in our movement and gesture, in our song and silence, in our music and poetic language, in what delights our eyes and our sense of smell, in how we arrange the space in which we worship, and in the form, shape, rhythm, and flow with which all of these elements combine as a whole. Spoken words are but one of the many languages of prayer. As Eugene Walsh observes in *Giving Life: The Ministry of the Parish Sunday Assembly* (Daytona Beach, Fla.: Pastoral Arts Associates, 1985), the ritual and ceremony we have inherited in the Judeo-Christian tradition call us to *gather* as a people of God;

to *listen* with our entire beings—as individuals and as a community—to God's word; and to *respond* to that word as Jesus Christ did, in total self-giving. We pray the Eucharist in order to become eucharist; to become persons and a people committed to giving our entire lives over to the way of God in the world.

To prepare liturgy means to prepare ourselves. For most of us, our first understanding of planning a liturgy was something akin to planning a curriculum. We started with an outline form, and we filled in the blanks and requirements according to a theme (often a one-word theme) that we found somewhere in the readings. Our recommendation here is that preparation needs to come *before* planning. We prepare ourselves, both students and teachers alike, by becoming familiar with the readings—by coming to own them. It is out of this living with the Scriptures that our planning flows.

Once plans are made, then each participant must be rehearsed in her or his role, whether as a member of the assembly or as lector, musician, cantor, presider, etc.

All preparations for liturgy begin with the liturgical season and the cycle of readings. We respond to seasons and to a yearly or cyclical way of moving through time. Granted, we struggle with the tension and complexity of so many conflicting calendars—the school year, the calendar year, the fiscal year, and nature's yearly seasons of winter, spring, summer, and fall. But the liturgical calendar need not conflict with the school calendar; rather, the liturgical calendar can be reflected in the school calendar and help to shape it.

For example, the weekday readings of Ordinary Time during early September usually present us with such questions as who is Jesus? what was he sent to do? what are we here on earth to do? to what are we called? With the beginning of the school year, we might go beyond focusing on newness of beginning—to a renewal of who we are called to be in Christ. In all that we do, we are to be disciples of Christ. In all of our studies, we seek to be formed in the ways of God.

1. The Basics_____

There are four basic areas of concern when preparing liturgy with students. If your situation or time doesn't permit any further preparations, the four areas that should be your main concern are (1) the readings, (2) music, (3) processions, and (4) environment.

THE READINGS

Look first to the readings of the day. Usually these will be the regular weekday readings of the Church calendar. These weekday readings are set up in a two-year cycle. The odd years (starting with Advent of the previous December) are Year One; the even years (likewise) are Year Two. Often you will also have the option of using the readings for a saint's day or a particular memorial or feast. These are listed by their calendar dates in the Lectionary table of contents.

We recommend that you check all the options and then choose the set of readings with which you are most comfortable before presenting the readings to the students. First check to see if the calendar date you have in mind is listed in the Lectionary table of contents. If the date is not listed, then use the readings for that day of the week in the liturgical year.

If the date is listed and is a solemnity, then the readings for the solemnity are to be used. If not listed as a solemnity but as a feast, then the readings for the feast are to be used. If not listed as a solemnity or a feast but as a memorial, you may wish to check an Ordo (the annually published official Church calendar) to determine whether the date is an optional or an obligatory memorial. For an obligatory memorial, the readings for the memorial are to be used if the date is not listed as a solemnity or a feast. For an optional memorial, you may choose between the memorial readings and the readings for the day of the week.

In short, solemnities take precedence over all other occasions, followed first by feasts, then by obligatory memorials, and finally by optional memorials and unclassified dates.

We highly recommend that every school make available a chapel-size Lectionary (book of readings) and a Sacramentary (book of prayers) for the use of teachers and students preparing for liturgy. Teachers and students might also appreciate having a Bible commentary to refer to for clarification of historical contexts or unusual words and titles.

Once you are ready to start discussing the readings with the students, we recommend that you not feed your own reflections to them. Let them chew and digest the readings for themselves. Ask them what meanings they find in the readings. Avoid making literal or definitive statements about what the word may or may not be saying. Let God's word speak for itself!

Also, rather than trying to find a theme in the readings, endeavor to connect what the word is saying with the meaning of Eucharist and an understanding of the Church as the people of God. Don't be "message" oriented.

Nor is it enough to just read the word. We encourage you to help students to live with the word, to relate it to their own experiences in life. Be story oriented. Let the students find themselves in the stories, prophecies, and exhortations. The word of God is an experience, not just a lesson. (See the U.S. bishops' document Directory for Masses with Children, nos. 41–49, entitled "Reading and Explanation of the Word of God.")

The next step is to convey your choice of readings to the presider and/or homilist well in advance of the liturgy in order to allow for preparation of the homily. You might also discuss the readings with the presider and/or homilist in order to coordinate and connect these reflections with your own and those of the students.

Lectors

The lectors chosen to proclaim the word at liturgy would best be those students (or teachers) who exhibit an understanding of the word, especially the word chosen to be read on a given day. At liturgy, we don't "read" the readings. The word of God is proclaimed. Proclamation requires that the lector understand and communicate God's presence in the word. (See The Constitution on the Sacred Liturgy, no. 7; General Instruction of the Roman Missal, no. 9; Lectionary for Mass: Introduction, no. 4).

In proclaiming, the lector expresses her or his faith in God's *active* presence in the word. "To proclaim" is "to speak boldly." Fr. Ed Hays, author of *Prayers for the Domestic Church* (Easton, Kans.: Forest of Peace Books, 1979), speaks of proclamation as addressing the word of God to the community for the sake of the world. This is no small potatoes! Children can speak boldly and proclaim with understanding if they are given time to reflect on the readings and if they are encouragingly supported in rehearsing them.

If proclamation is to speak to the mind, to the soul, and to the entire being, then time needs to be allowed for a meditative silence after each reading. The lector should be rehearsed in how to handle such moments of silence. When the same person is handling both the first reading and the psalm, he or she might simply step back one step from the ambo (lectern) after proclaiming the first reading, bow his or her head, and count slowly to ten (without moving the lips) before continuing with the psalm.

If, however, a separate cantor or psalm leader is available—a practice we would encourage—then the lector sits down directly after proclaiming the word. Once the lector is seated, the cantor or psalm leader counts to ten before rising for the psalm. The responsorial psalm is not a proclamation; it is itself a response to the first reading, so no silence is required after the psalm.

Book Bearer

To focus further attention on the word, if an opening procession is used the lector or another student might act as book bearer in the procession. The book should be held high above the head and held firmly with both hands. If the book weighs more than the student does(!) it might be carried by two students holding it on high.

The walk in procession is not an ordinary walk. The book bearer carries the powerful symbol of the presence of God among us in the word. Posture, movement, and expression should reflect a cherished reverence for this bold and powerful symbol.

General Intercessions

Included in the Liturgy of the Word and directly connected to a spirit of full, conscious, and active listening and responding to the word of God are the general intercessions, also known as the prayers of the faithful or prayers of petition. This prayer form, used by members of the early Church, had fallen out of use over the centuries, but it has been reintroduced in the recent reforms of the liturgy. The general intercessions are publicly spoken prayers, written and led by members of the assembly.

At student liturgies, these prayers should be rooted in the language and experience of the students and should be appropriate to the age level of the students praying them. The instructions of the U.S. bishops for the general intercessions remind us that these prayers should reflect the needs of the assembly—as well as the needs of the universal Church—and that they should be rooted in a response to the readings.

We must remember that no assembly ever stands alone but gathers with the entire people of God throughout time and space as part of the universal Church under the reign of God. Our general intercessions, therefore, start by praying for the whole of creation: the world and the Church, all leaders and all people. Our petitions then move progressively through the more local needs of our community at its various levels to those of the gathered assembly, all the while reflecting on the word being proclaimed at the liturgy. Since Christ always showed special concern for the poor, the downtrodden, and those relegated to the margins of society, our prayers of petition always do well to remember the needs of these people.

Please note: The intercessions provided in various printed resources may be used as models or examples, but the petitions prayed at each liturgy should come from the heart and speak with the voice of that assembly.

One further concern is that the student or teacher who leads these prayers be prepared. It would be best if this person received a copy of the prayers a few days in advance of the liturgy to allow time to pray them personally. In so doing, the prayer leader might come to make the prayers her or his own and, therefore, be better able to lead the assembly in prayer. Reciting does not encourage others to pray. Praying does!

MUSIC

The choice of music for sung prayer should reflect the insights and responses that flow from the students' Scripture reflections.

The Acclamations

When selecting the sung prayer to be used at liturgy, look first to the acclamations. There are four acclamations in our liturgy:

Gospel acclamation
Holy, holy
Eucharistic acclamation
Great Amen

An acclamation is a type of prayer. It is intended to be sung. In the U.S. bishops' document Music in Catholic Worship, an acclamation is defined as a "shout of joy!" A shout of joy is most fully expressed through a bursting forth into song from the heart. If nothing else in the liturgy is sung, these four moments are intended to be songs of praise that call for the entire assembly to join in singing.

If either Eucharistic Prayer II or III for Masses with Children is used, additional acclamations are provided. These additional responses are in the same spirit of prayer as the acclamations just mentioned, and they, too, should be sung.

It is helpful to have a person or group of persons act as leaders of song in order to focus the attention of the assembly and encourage its collective participation. Such leaders need to be people who are musically confident. Their role is to enable our sung prayer, not to distract us or to entertain us or to amuse us. They serve their purpose best, however, when they are clearly visible to the assembly.

Song of Gathering

If you are able to incorporate music beyond the acclamations, the next musical priority in the liturgy is the song of gathering. This song is generally to be a song of praise. It serves three purposes: (1) to reflect the spirit of the liturgical season, (2) to accompany the procession through the worship space, and (3) most crucially of all, to gather us together as a worshiping community.

Our individual selves are integrated into a community of worship as the entire assembly breaks forth together into song. The song of gathering needs to last long enough to enable some felt experience of the community having joined together.

Communion Song

Our time of Communion also calls for communal singing. The form of song that tends to engage us most effectively here is either responsorial (where the choir or cantor sings the verses of a song-form hymn and the assembly joins in on each refrain) or a short, repetitive refrain or mantra (in the style of Taizé, for example). These musical forms free us from the distraction of books and papers. The Communion song is intended to reinforce our union—Com-union—in Christ and with one another. Such song forms move with and enhance our sense of procession, of movement together. The Communion song is not to be "tacked on" toward the end of our time for Communion, nor is it to be sung after Communion.

Here, then, for quick reference is an outline of the basic musical moments in our liturgy that call for the entire assembly to join in singing before any other musical moments are added. The outline is drawn from the document Music in Catholic Worship.

> ***The acclamations***
> Gospel acclamation
> Holy, holy
> Eucharistic acclamation
> Great Amen
> ***Song of gathering***
> ***Communion song***

The document also includes the doxology of the Lord's Prayer as an acclamation ("For the kingdom, the power . . .") but suggests that this is best sung only if the Lord's Prayer itself is sung.

All other hymn singing in our liturgy is supplementary. For a time after the reforms of the Second Vatican Council many assemblies became trapped in what musicians affectionately refer to as the "four-hymn syndrome." We borrowed anthem singing from Protestant liturgies and tried to incorporate it in our ritual. But our liturgy is shaped differently. The focal musical moments of our liturgy call for the entire assembly to join in singing the acclamations, a song of gathering, and a repetitive Communion mantra or refrain. All other possible musical moments in our liturgy are secondary to these.

PROCESSIONS

Walking in procession is more than just an ordinary walk.

Gathering Procession

Serious consideration should be given to the use of a gathering procession as a beginning to prayer. Our walking in the gathering procession can be a prayer in itself that carries our whole being closer to God. Procession symbolizes our moving toward God, our moving from our everyday lives and situations into a sacred space. Our church—wherever it is—is a holy place, a place where we come to meet our God in each other, in God's word, and in the sharing of Eucharist. As Church, we engage in this meeting with our God at once both more intimately and more formally (in that our communal prayer has structure or form to it) than we will often have occasion to do in our everyday lives.

A gathering procession could include all ministers (presider, lector, musicians, petition readers, servers) and even the entire assembly. The Lectionary, candles, and processional cross could be carried by students who will not necessarily be the altar servers. Remind the students that these objects are being employed for extraordinary—beyond the ordinary—purposes and therefore are to be handled in extraordinary ways.

Procession with the Gifts

The procession with and presentation of the gifts (formerly known as the offertory procession) requires some clarification. The focus of attention at this time is not on the people in the procession, nor is it on the offering of ourselves. The offering of ourselves in the liturgy is a process that begins at our gathering and culminates with our action of sharing in the Body and Blood of Christ. When we say "Amen" at Communion time we are saying, "Yes, we will be like Christ and give ourselves over completely to the challenge—as well as the comfort—of his love."

The focus of attention during the procession with the gifts is on the procession itself, which symbolizes our movement to the Eucharistic table. We move to the table with gifts "made by human hands"—the bread and the wine. These gifts are ordinary, everyday objects, which Jesus Christ changed for us forever into extraordinary gifts of love. In like fashion, we ordinary people are called to be transformed into extraordinary gifts of love for one another and for all of God's creation by the power of God's moving presence in our lives.

No other symbols need be brought in procession aside from the bread and the wine (not even a cruet of water!). These simple gifts might be carried with arms raised so that the objects—the symbols—are clearly visible. As mentioned earlier, a walk in procession is no ordinary walk. Walking, here, is yet another everyday gift transformed at liturgy into the extraordinary.

Something else to keep in mind: As the U.S. bishops' document Environment and Art in Catholic Worship reminds us, the vessels need to look like they hold bread and wine. The integrity of these vessels needs to reflect the integrity of the substances they contain.

The option also exists of not having a procession with the gifts. In this case, the presider simply prepares the table and uses the beautiful blessing prayers, which may be spoken aloud ("Blessed are you, Lord God of all creation . . ."). These words and his gestures focus our attention appropriately on the humble gifts of bread and wine brought before the Lord, and on our gathering around the Eucharistic table.

ENVIRONMENT

Providing environment for our worship encompasses more than just providing visual art or decoration for our worship space. The time and energy spent in preparation for liturgy helps to create the atmosphere or environment for our prayer, for it is during this time of preparation that our prayer begins to take shape and gain meaning for us. Rehearsal and preparation require a discipline that calls us beyond where we are, in order more fully to engage us in prayer.

We cannot make anyone pray. We can only work together to create a welcoming and comfortable environment in which people might feel the yearning to open their hearts and minds and whole lives to God.

The sign of peace is an integral part of this reverent and hospitable sensitivity in liturgy. In offering one another a gesture of peace we demonstrate our commitment to be like Christ in all that we do. With this outward sign we pray that we will be strengthened in our efforts to move beyond the barriers that keep us from fully loving one another.

Visual art can help create an environment for worship. We need, however, to ask a two-pronged question when considering any form of visual addition: Are the visuals going to clutter either the time of preparation or the worship space, or are they going to be used in a way that will engage us in the process of prayer? Oftentimes a creative visual addition to the worship space is neither necessary nor called for. Undertaking the creation of such works might, therefore, best be reserved for occasions when time abounds or when there is a special season or feast to be celebrated.

One practice with a visual impact that is often overlooked is the use of loose papers. If the students are reading general intercessions from loose sheets of paper, perhaps these could be mounted on individual matting boards to be carried by the students, or the papers could be placed in a notebook or folder.

The use of missalettes also has an impact on our worship environment. These aids are of a temporary character. They are printed on low quality paper and are disposable. Missalettes should therefore never be used for the proclamation of God's word at liturgy. The lector should always proclaim from the Lectionary or from an attractively covered notebook.

Altar servers may or may not be used at a given liturgy. But whenever students do act as altar servers, they should be trained so that they can be at ease with their role. How they move can help us in our prayer. The ease and beauty and attentiveness of their actions and gestures can further invite and engage us all in participation.

The Basics

For liturgy organizers

Liturgical season _____

Date_____ Day_____ Time_____

PREPARING. Look first to the readings of the day.

Choice of Readings
First reading _____
Psalm _____
Gospel _____

Personal Reflection on the above Scripture passages.

Daily Scripture Reflection on the above passages with students in class. We recommend that you also discuss these Scripture passages with whoever is to preside and/or offer the homily at your liturgy, sharing with that person the students' reflections as well as your own.

PLANNING. This flows from reflection on the readings.

Lector _____

Choose from among the students a lector who exhibits an understanding of the Scripture readings. Rehearse with the student until he or she is able to convey effectively both the words and the powerful presence of Christ in the words.

General Intercessions: Ask the students what they perceive to be the needs of the earth, of their nation, of their Church, of their community, of the poor and outcast, of their school, of the students in their class. These needs are to connect with the Scripture passages of the day and are meant to call us to love, justice, and peace in God's reign. Jot down the students' thoughts, and then have one or more of the students put these expressed needs into written form. Choose a student to lead the prayer of the general intercessions, and rehearse with the student until he or she comes to an understanding of the prayers.

Leader_____

Music: Have the students select the musical settings they would prefer to use for the acclamations. Ask them which of the variable Eucharistic acclamations, what song of gathering, and what Communion song might reflect the mood and experience they have found in the readings.

Song of gathering _____

Gospel acclamation _____

Holy, holy _____

Eucharistic acclamation _____

Great Amen _____

Communion Song _____

Gathering Procession ☐ Yes   ☐ No

Origin of procession _____

Route of procession_____

Cross bearer _____

Candle bearers _____

_____

Book bearer _____

If you choose to have a gathering procession, decide with the students where it will begin, what route it will take, and whether candles will be carried. Also decide who will carry the cross and who will carry the book. Rehearse the procession with those involved (including altar servers, below).

Procession with the Gifts ☐ Yes   ☐ No

Gift bearers _____

_____

If you decide to have a procession with the gifts, choose two students to carry the bread and wine in procession. Rehearse with them the way in which they will hold the vessels as well as the manner of their walk.

Altar Servers _____

_____

Choose an altar server or two, if you have students trained and prepared for this role.

Discuss all of the above with the presider, and give him a copy of *The Musical Basics* form, or the *Beyond the Basics* form for a more elaborate liturgy. Any others involved in the liturgy should receive a copy of the same form. The music teacher/coordinator should receive the *Beyond the Musical Basics* form for a more elaborate liturgy. A copy of the general intercessions should be given to the presider/homilist as well as copies of any readings that have been adapted and any other special instructions.

The Musical Basics
For presiders, coordinators, and music leaders

Liturgical season _____

Date_____ Day_____ Time_____

Gathering Procession ☐ Yes ☐ No

    Origin of procession _____

    Route of procession_____

    Participants: Cross bearer _____

             Candle bearers _____

             _____

             Book bearer _____

153,042

Altar servers _____

_____

Homilist _____

Presider _____

Song of Gathering _____

Gospel Acclamation _____

Procession with the Gifts: ☐ Yes   ☐ No

Eucharistic Prayer _____

Holy, Holy _____

Eucharistic Acclamation _____

Other Acclamations (for use with Eucharistic Prayers for Masses with Children)

_____

Great Amen _____

Communion Song _____

*These moments are to be your first musical priorities in the liturgy. They call for singing *by the entire assembly* before any other musical moments are added.

2. Beyond the Basics_____

If your situation allows more time for preparation and more involvement on the part of the students, consider the following ideas for further developing these four main areas of concern from "The Basics" section, plus two other areas of concern:

1. Proclamation of the word
2. Further musical involvement
3. Gospel procession
4. Environment and art
5. The presidential prayers
6. Rhythm and flow

PROCLAMATION OF THE WORD

Proclamation can be handled in any of the following ways:

One lector proclaims the reading.

Divided Reading, where two or three students divide the reading by paragraph or sentence. This should be done only if the reading lends itself to such a setting or division of voices.

Dialogue form or dramatization involving a group of students. This can be done with the first reading and/or the gospel (the latter, if the presider is open to the form). The dramatization can simply be a spoken presentation of the reading by the various characters involved in it, or it can involve any combination of mime, dance, props, staging, or costumes. Any such dramatization must be carefully prepared so that the assembly is engaged in the word, not just entertained by it.

Just a word of caution regarding commentary. Spoken commentary is not an integral part of the liturgy. It was introduced with the advent of liturgical reforms in order to guide the assembly through the renewed form of our worship. By this point, however, we generally no longer require such instruction.

At present, commentary is most often used as an introduction before Mass and before the first and second readings. But adding these additional words to our liturgical prayer imposes a language of explanation on the liturgy rather than allowing the languages of symbolism and action, so essential to the liturgy, to speak for themselves. You need not feel obliged to write any commentary. Indeed, perhaps we can work toward helping students to *experience* God, rather than trying always to teach them *about* God. Perhaps we can bring students, outside of the context of the liturgy itself, to understand—and to do—liturgy so well that we won't need commentary to explain what we are doing or what we are about.

Once you have effectively prepared and planned for prayer, use commentary only if you feel the need for further clarification of context or of Old Testament imagery. Even these purposes, however, are often better served if the observations are incorporated in the homily. Commentaries are not meant to be miniature homilies.

First preparing and then planning liturgy can lead to an experience of liturgical prayer at which there is no need for commentary. There may be occasions when you choose to use an introduction at the beginning of the liturgy as part of the gathering ritual, in order to create a desired mood or atmosphere for worship. Our word of caution is simply that commentary should be used sparingly if at all and should be carefully written when it is used.

FURTHER MUSICAL INVOLVEMENT

In "The Basics" section we offered a list of musical moments in the liturgy that are to be given priority:

The acclamations
Gospel acclamation
Holy, holy
Eucharistic acclamation
Great Amen
Song of gathering
Communion song

Here we extend that list with a discussion of further musical involvement. The following musical moments are to be added only if you have an assembly that is already singing at the above mentioned moments, and only if you have the musical resources and personnel to make these moments truly sung prayer.

Responsorial Psalm

Psalms are songs. They were written as lyrics, poetic texts intended to be sung. The voice of the psalmist often speaks with an emotionally charged fervor, employing stark imagery. As a result, this prayer form can be difficult to follow when it is simply spoken. It is much more readily accessible when it is sung.

You might consider inviting some of the students to train as cantors or song leaders for various liturgies throughout the year.

Cantors pray the sung verses of the psalm and gospel acclamation and lead the assembly in their response to the psalm and in the gospel acclamation. If the general intercessions are sung, the cantor also prays these and leads the assembly in their response to the petitions. The cantor prays on behalf of the assembly.

Song leaders lead the assembly in sung prayer at other times in the liturgy.

These two roles in the leadership of sung prayer can be performed by one student or by two separate students.

Occasional and Seasonal Music

Depending on the Scripture of the day and on the liturgical season, you might consider some of the following options for sung prayer:

Penitential Rite. The penitential rite could be sung during the penitential season of Lent, using a musical setting whose mood might call the students to a deeper internal search for repentance. There are three forms for the penitential rite from which to choose.

First form. The presider invites those assembled to recall their own times of sinfulness and to pray for mercy together in silence. The silence is followed by the *Confiteor* (''I confess to almighty God . . .''), which is then followed by the ''Lord, have mercy.''

Second form. The second form proceeds in dialogue prayer as follows:

Presider: Lord, we have sinned against you.
Lord, have mercy.
Assembly: Lord, have mercy.
Presider: Lord, show us your mercy and love.
Assembly: And grant us your salvation.
Presider: May almighty God have mercy on us, forgive us our sins, and bring us to everlasting life.
Assembly: Amen.

Third form. The third form consists of three invocations prayed by the presider, to each of which the assembly responds. The Sacramentary offers eight sets of invocations from which to choose. Example:

Presider: You raise the dead to life in the Spirit.
Lord, have mercy.
Assembly: Lord, have mercy.
Presider: You bring pardon and peace to the sinner.
Christ, have mercy.
Assembly: Christ, have mercy.

Presider: You bring light to those in darkness.
Lord, have mercy.
Assembly: Lord, have mercy.

In place of any one of these forms, a rite of blessing and sprinkling with holy water may be used. This ritual, the *asperges*, reminds us of the new life into which we have been born through our baptism and is detailed in the Sacramentary. The *asperges* may also be accompanied by a musical setting of the "Lord, have mercy."

Some communities have taken up the practice of writing their own texts for the penitential rite. Before choosing such an option, we recommend you consider using one of the texts for this prayer available in the Sacramentary. If none of these texts suits the students' objectives, then you may have students model their prayer after the third form, making sure they maintain both the form and the spirit of the prayer, whether spoken or sung. Notice that the penitential invocations focus on God's generous mercy, rather than on our sinfulness. This prayer is intended to be short, and time for silent reflection should always be taken after each invocation or after the entire prayer.

Glory to God. This prayer is a song of joy and praise that follows the penitential rite at Sunday Eucharist. The "Glory to God" can be sung—occasionally—at a weekday liturgy during the festive seasons of Christmas and Easter. A responsorial setting of this hymn of praise might best engage the whole assembly in the song.

General Intercessions. If the students are prepared to take particular care in preparing to sing them, the general intercessions may be sung at liturgy. It would be especially appropriate to have these prayers of petition sung at liturgies during the seasons of Advent, when we pray for the "becoming" of God's reign in the world, or Lent, when we pray for the "repairing" of God's reign. The intercessions could be sung by a student cantor, who would then lead the assembly in a response to each intercession. The form would resemble that used for the responsorial psalm. A period of silence should follow each intercession, preceding the response, whether the prayer is sung or spoken. Example:

That we may always endeavor to listen to others,
and to love them even in their differences *from* us,

Let us pray to *the* Lord.　　　　　　Lord, hear our prayer.

Lamb of God. The "Lamb of God," which accompanies the fraction rite (the breaking of the bread), could be sung when Eucharistic ministers are used or when Communion under both forms is to be shared. On either of these occasions, the fraction rite—a time of preparation for the sharing of Communion—involves more ceremony and could be enhanced with the addition of music.

The Lord's Prayer and doxology ("For the kingdom . . .") could be sung at liturgies attended by students who are just learning the Lord's Prayer, or at liturgies during Advent when the image of the reign of God plays such a prominent role in our seasonal Scripture readings.

If you do choose to sing the Lord's Prayer, be sure to select a simple setting that encourages the entire assembly to join in the singing.

If the Lord's Prayer is sung, it is best that the doxology also be sung, and vice versa.

Supplementary Music

Procession with the Gifts. A mantra-like hymn or a song-form hymn sung antiphonally between the choir (or cantor) and the assembly could accompany the procession with the gifts. Our focus of attention here is on the symbolic action of movement to the Eucharistic table. Any music used here should support and enhance this main action. It should never distract us from watching and being inwardly involved in the beauty of this ceremony as we see the procession unfold, the gifts presented, and the table prepared. The use of instrumental or choral music at this time might, therefore, be most appropriate of all.

Recessional. A recessional song, if used, should support the enthusiasm and inspiration of the concluding rites of our prayer, which encourage us to go forth and bring eucharist to the world; to endeavor always to be more Christlike; to participate in the ever becoming of the reign of God.

Some Final Notes on Music

Three Musical Forms. At present, we have three primary forms of music from which to choose. We highly recommend you make an effort throughout the year to include all three of these sung prayer forms. By doing so you help to broaden the prayer experience of students.

Musical prayer forms serve as expressive elements of our liturgy that help to shape and expand our image of, and feelings about, our God. We need to take them very seriously.

Through-Composed Hymns. A through-composed hymn consists of full verses without a refrain and generally employs a poetic text. Example: "Praise to the Lord, the Almighty."

Song-Form Hymns. A song-form hymn uses verses with a recurring refrain or response. It is often sung antiphonally between choir (or cantor) and assembly. The text may be either scripturally based or poetic. Example: "Sing a New Song" by Dan Schutte, S.J. (*Glory and Praise* 1. Phoenix: North American Liturgy Resources).

Mantra-Like Hymns. A mantra-like hymn uses repetition of a short text set to a simple melody. This form was initiated by

Music from Taizé in France. Example: "Eat This Bread" by Jacques Berthier (*Music from Taizé,* vol. 2. Chicago: G.I.A. Publications).

Compiling a Common Repertoire List. Your school might consider having each teacher submit a list of acclamations, Mass part settings, and hymns that her or his class knows and can pray well. These classroom lists could be compiled into a common repertoire list, possibly categorized by season. The students responsible for planning a given liturgy could then make their musical selections from this list.

Having a common repertoire list could facilitate greater participation at liturgy and better communication in planning it.

Using Movement and Gesture. We recommend, particularly with younger ones, that movement and gesture occasionally be incorporated in the students' sung prayer. For example, you might let the whole class process into the liturgy singing the song of gathering; use uplifted arms and hand clapping to further engage the students in the acclamations; use a full pattern of hand and arm movements, possibly even holding vigil candles, to accompany the gospel acclamation; invite all the students to use the American sign language gesture for "Alleluia" during the gospel acclamation; rehearse the students' Communion procession while having them sing their Communion song; and rehearse the students in whatever manner they choose for sharing Communion, whether in the hand or on the tongue.

Memorizing Music. Children as well as adults will tend to pray more attentively if they are free of paper in their hands and words to read. For collectively spoken or sung prayer, the use of memorized or short, simple texts serves best, eliminating the need for printed participation aids.

GOSPEL PROCESSION

A gospel procession is another form of movement prayer that can be used at worship. It involves a procession with the book held high and includes any number of processional- or vigil-candle bearers. Such a procession would begin at the altar, where the book would be picked up, and move around the worship space accompanied by the singing of an extended gospel acclamation. The book would then be brought to the ambo (lectern) or placed in the hands of the presider.

Such a procession would probably be best reserved for festive occasions during the year.

ENVIRONMENT AND ART

Artistic Expression

When we come together to worship God, we bring our various cultural, ethnic, and aesthetic backgrounds with us. These living backgrounds that so shape who we are can be incorporated in artistic expressions of our faith. When liturgically and prayerfully centered, carefully planned and executed, effective artistic expressions can generate a life-giving force in our liturgies that transforms us in the experience. These expressions can help to send us out into the world revitalized for the work of building God's reign of justice, peace, and love.

Before it is anything else, visual art is experiential, not cognitive. We encourage you, therefore, to resist the temptation to incorporate words in the art you use or create. We pray preconceptually with visual art. We pray with colors, lines, and shapes rather than with words. Good art should reveal something about us, our interests and feelings. Student art often depicts their Christian lives in forms and images that are untraditional, fresh, and full of vitality. Such qualities can engage the imaginations of adults and students alike.

By exploring with students a wide range of possibilities for visual images dealing with the journey of faith, you introduce them to new opportunities for creative prayer. By allowing students to express their faith artistically, you encourage the creative thinking process and hands-on experience that will foster their deeper understandings and reinforce their faith. The use of student art in liturgy allows the artists involved an active participation in their worship.

Craft Work

Especially with younger students—though this applies to all—it is vital that the criteria used for craftwork be appropriate to the age and abilities of the individual student. Establishing criteria requires striking a delicate balance between stretching a student's understanding (an essential focal point of our work) and affirming the student's endeavors (an essential dynamic of our ministry).

We do well to keep in mind that the very nature of art involves a *search* for beauty. In the overall learning process, the love and care, enthusiasm and spirit, with which an art work is accomplished can manifest beauty more eloquently than the finished product.

Liturgical Appropriateness

Good liturgy demands that any art we use at liturgy be appropriate and conducive to our communal worship. This applies whether the art is designed to enhance the worship space, the ritual actions, or the symbolic objects to be used. To this end, student art often does well to focus on one or a few select aspects of a given feast or season of the liturgical year.

The purpose of using any form of art in the liturgy is not to entertain us. Liturgically appropriate artistic expression draws us into deeper reflection on the word or on the ways in which the Eucharist shapes us into a people of God in Christ. You might use this as a simple litmus test for the liturgical suitability of any artistic expression, whatever form it takes.

Generally, artistic enhancements of a worship space are best reserved for use on special occasions.

Seasonal Colors

Traditionally, the colors for the seasons of the Church year have been blue violet for Advent, red violet for Lent, white for Christmas and Easter, and green for Ordinary Time. The use of seasonal colors helps us visually to connect with the rhythm of cycles in our prayer.

Highlighting Liturgical Focal Points

The focal points of our attention at liturgy are the following:

Assembly
Table of the word
Table of the Eucharist
Baptismal font
Book
Vessels
Presider

At every liturgy the dignity of each individual member of the assembly, as reflected by posture, movement, attitude, and dress, is a part of our prayer, a part of what we bring to God. Aware that our bodies are holy temples of the Lord, we bring to worship the entirety of who we are, as well as the promise of who we are called to become. When it gathers, the assembly becomes something greater than the sum of its individual members. It becomes a prayer offering in itself that joins with the whole Church throughout time and space—and indeed with the whole of creation—in praising God.

Once the vital role of the assembly at liturgy has been made clear to students—and has been experienced by them—perhaps they can be encouraged to dress in a manner that reflects their regard for the role they play as part of the assembly. They might also better understand why their demeanor at liturgy is to be reverent and prayerful.

If the students with whom you are working seek expression in visual creativity as a result of their reflection on given Scripture passages, you might consider some of the following suggestions:

The table of the word (the ambo or lectern), the table of the Eucharist (the altar), and the book (the Lectionary) could each be decorated with some form of visually coordinated fabric art.

Environment and Art in Catholic Worship reminds us that the decoration of any object in the liturgy should never overwhelm the object itself. The integrity of the object must always be respected.

If the Scripture for either a given day or for the liturgical season calls us to remember the living waters of our baptism, the baptismal font area could become a focal point of attention, enlivened with living plants or flowers. The students could participate in decorating the area by each bringing a garden flower to a given liturgy and placing it with everyone else's in one big, beautiful bouquet at the baptismal font. This could be done informally before the liturgy starts, or it could be done in a processional ceremony, followed by a sprinkling of the assembly with the baptismal waters of the font. Such a ceremony could take place at the time of the penitential rite or immediately following a homily that might be devoted in part to an explanation of this symbolic action.

The vessels used in the liturgy cannot readily be decorated or enhanced visually. Their shape, color, and substance are what they are. But having students carry the vessels—as also the book—held boldly on high during any procession with these objects can help to dramatize the power and importance of these symbols in our liturgy.

Students can also be invited to prepare the altar for the Eucharist. Just before the procession with the gifts, two or three students can place the linens and the Sacramentary on the table. Such participation needs to be well choreographed and rehearsed.

The vestment worn by the presider is also a part of our prayer environment. The students might consider crafting some sort of appliqué that could be applied—either permanently or temporarily—to a presider's vestment being made by the parish community or to one that the parish already owns. This could be undertaken as a long-term school project, with different appliqués designed for various school and liturgical occasions.

Banners

What about banners? Banners can serve to make a statement or to create a mood. Because liturgy can be prone to wordiness, we recommend that banners be allowed to make their statements and create their moods without the use of words. This can be accomplished through the thoughtful use of images, symbols, and shapes. Careful preparation would therefore involve discussing with the students what different symbols and images mean for them and for us as a community of faith.

Traditionally, banners attached to poles have been used to enhance the movement and reflect the character of a procession, whether it be joyful or somber. Color, in and of itself, can be very effective in creating a mood. The banners you might use in a procession could be as simple as ribbon streamers or strips of colored fabric hung from a horizontal piece of wood mounted atop a pole.

When a banner is attached to a wall or suspended from the ceiling, we refer to it as a hanging. A hanging should respect and enhance the integrity of the total worship space. It would be best that it be constructed of durable materials so it has a look of permanency about it and could be used again.

Having students submit color draft designs for their banners or hangings before they start constructing them can facilitate discussion about what will and will not work in a given space. Ask yourself and them if the banner might clutter rather than enhance the space. Does a given wall need to be covered? Is the banner distracting? Is it engaging?

Symbols

Symbols draw us beyond themselves as gateways to deeper insights into reality. They operate on many different levels within our conscious and unconscious minds. Before all else, they operate in the realm of our imaginations, a realm within which young students move freely and easily.

Liturgical symbols conjure up for us a wealth of associations that are, at once, both personal and communal in nature. These symbols continually call us to deeper understandings, and to an ever-expanding sense of appreciation for the mysteries we seek to touch. Consider some of the many ways in which the following objects serve as symbols within our faith tradition:

Candles symbolize the triumph of light over darkness; life consumed in the flame of God's love; the presence of that which is holy and untouchable . . .

Incense symbolizes our prayer rising to God; the sacrifice of our lives returned to God (echoing the sacrifice of animals in Hebrew tradition to pay homage to God) . . .

Water symbolizes cleansing and refreshment; the quenching of our thirsts; the empowerment for growth . . .

The cross symbolizes Christ's victory over death and the forces of evil; the meeting of the human and the divine in the life, death, and resurrection of Christ . . .

Bread symbolizes our spiritual nourishment; the life-giving nature of our faith; the reality that only when we recognize our brokenness can we truly become one with one another and with our God . . .

Wine symbolizes the vitality of Christ's loving presence in the world passed on to us to enliven our entire beings, even as does the blood that courses through our veins; the abandonment with which we are invited to lose ourselves in God; the jubilation our rapturous love for God promises, especially in the context of a communal celebration of that love, as at a banquet or wedding feast . . .

We also believe that in the symbolic *action* of breaking bread and sharing wine in remembrance of Christ, the real presence of Christ is manifest in our midst as we become one body with one another in and through Christ. This is our Communion.

All of these symbols speak to our senses as well as to our minds. Allowing students to experience each of these object-symbols as part of their prayer at various times throughout the year can help to engage the students in full, conscious, and active prayer.

THE PRESIDENTIAL PRAYERS

The presidential prayers are those prayers spoken by the presider on behalf of the entire assembly. They include the following:

Opening prayer
Prayer over the gifts
Eucharistic Prayer
Prayer after Communion

If the presider is open to such involvement, after the students have come to an understanding of the readings for a given liturgy they might be interested in selecting the presidential prayers to be used in the liturgy.

Except for the Eucharistic Prayer, the presidential prayers for a given weekday of the Church year are determined, as are the Lectionary readings, by whether the date is (1) a solemnity, (2) a feast, (3) an obligatory or optional memorial, or (4) unclassified. Once again, solemnities take precedence over all other occasions, followed first by feasts, then by obligatory memorials, and finally by optional memorials and unclassified dates.

We can become more fully engaged in our prayer at liturgy by familiarizing ourselves with the presidential prayers for the liturgy. These prayers can also often enhance our understanding of the readings for the day.

There are four standard Eucharistic Prayers and three Eucharistic Prayers specifically written for Masses where children make up most of the assembly. The latter three prayers are written in a language more readily understood by younger students. They also incorporate more acclamations than do the four standard Eucharistic Prayers. If one of the three Eucharistic Prayers for children is to be used, it must be carefully rehearsed by students and presider alike.

There are also two Eucharistic Prayers for times of reconciliation. These prayers make use of a beautiful poetic language that calls us to reconcile divisions among ourselves, even as Christ reconciles us with God. These prayers can be especially appropriate for specific occasions and are perhaps best used with older students.

RHYTHM AND FLOW

Within the Liturgy

Our liturgical prayer is like a work of art. When all of the elements come together, a rhythm and flow is created. In the interest of carefully shaping that rhythm and flow, we would encourage students and teachers to consider the following suggestions:

Movement. Be deliberate and reverently full of care in all movement and gesture.

Silence. Remember to allow for the prayer of silence, especially before the Liturgy of the Word begins, after the first reading, after the homily, and after the sharing of Communion.

Pace. Never rush. Move with a slow and gentle pace in a graceful, fluid line. There is a definite sense in which our prayer is choreographed!

Maintaining Focus. Avoid doing anything that might distract the assembly from its primary action at a given moment. For example, during the sharing of Communion the focus of attention is on the assembly moving together as one body in Christ. To invite the assembly at this point to sing a hymn from a book draws their attention to the hymnal and the printed lyrics and away from their experience of the procession as an act that unites them with one another in Christ. We are called at this moment to sing in a way that supports our "Communion." The use of a repetitive mantra, antiphonal refrain, or a memorized hymn can effectively enhance this vital liturgical moment, whereas the use of printed materials can often obscure it.

Pivotal Moments. Pay special attention to the following pivotal moments in our liturgy:

Gathering song and procession
Gospel
Eucharistic Prayer
Sharing in Communion
"Go forth" dismissal

All other actions flow to or from these moments.

Within the Liturgical Year

Our liturgical year and the cycle of readings in the Lectionary also have a profound influence on the rhythm and flow of our liturgies.

Scheduling Masses. To tap into the rhythm of the liturgical year, you might want to consider scheduling school or class Masses so that they correspond to the liturgical season and feasts rather than the calendar year. With careful study, you might even discover that certain readings or feasts would correlate well with the religion curriculum for a particular grade or class, so that the corresponding liturgy could be prepared for and planned by that group.

Daily or weekly prayer might employ the Liturgy of the Hours format (see section 3 of this book).

Class Planning. It might take some extra time to look at the readings for an extended period and to make long-term preparations; but undertaking such a discipline might provide a rich opportunity for adult faith development for teachers. This might prove especially the case if several teachers gathered to work on the project together, sharing their Scripture reflections and faith journey with one another in the process.

Seasonal Acclamation Settings. We can also tune into the rhythm of the liturgical seasons by changing the musical set-

153,0 42

tings we use for the acclamations whenever we move into a new liturgical season. These settings could be used throughout the given season, even on a recurring basis from year to year, and would then come to be associated with that season. For example, a more pensive setting could be used during Lent, and the interconnection between Christmas and Easter could be emphasized by using the same festive settings of the acclamations for both seasons. Selecting a Eucharistic Prayer could also be done by season.

Rhythm, then, is not just a musical element. It is a vital part of our lives. Recognizing and tuning into its cycles can help us appreciate the flow of interconnections in all that we do as we move through time.

Beyond the Basics

For presiders and coordinators

(*Complete this form only* **after** *having completed* **The Basics** *form.*)

Liturgical season _____

Date_____ Day_____ Time_____

Gathering Procession □ Yes   □ No

    Origin of procession _____

    Route of procession_____

    Participants: Cross bearer _____

              Candle bearers _____

                          _____

              Book bearer _____

Altar servers _____

_____

Homilist _____
Presider _____

Song of Gathering _____
Song leader _____

Penitential Rite Form_____ ☐ Sung ☐ Spoken

Glory to God: ☐ Sung ☐ Spoken

Opening Prayer: Sacramentary page _____

First Reading _____ Lectionary page _____
☐ One lector ☐ Divided reading ☐ Dialogue form
Lector(s) _____

_____

Responsorial Psalm _____
Cantor_____

Gospel Procession: ☐ Yes ☐ No
Origin of procession _____
Route of procession_____
Participants: Candle bearers _____

_____

Book bearer _____

*Gospel Acclamation _____

Gospel: _____ Lectionary page _____
☐ Presider ☐ Deacon
☐ Divided Reading ☐ Dialogue Form
Proclaimer(s) _____

_____

General Intercessions (attach written petitions to this form)
Led by_____ ☐ Sung ☐ Spoken
Response_____ ☐ Sung ☐ Spoken

Procession with the Gifts ☐ Yes ☐ No

    Origin of procession _____

    Route of procession_____

    Music _____

    Persons carrying the gifts _____

    _____

Prayer over the Gifts: Sacramentary page _____

Eucharistic Prayer _____

**Holy, Holy*_____

**Eucharistic Acclamation*_____

*Other Acclamations (for use with Eucharistic Prayers for Masses with Children)

    _____

*Great Amen _____

Lord's Prayer and Doxology ☐ Sung ☐ Spoken

Lamb of God: ☐ Sung ☐ Spoken

Communion Under Both Forms ☐ Yes ☐ No

**Communion Song*_____

Prayer After Communion Sacramentary page _____

Recessional Song _____

OTHER CONSIDERATIONS:

Visuals and Their Locations

    _____

    _____

Commentary: When _____

                 Read by _____

*These moments are to be your first musical priorities in the liturgy. They call for singing *by the entire assembly* before any other musical moments are added.

Beyond the Musical Basics
For music leaders

Liturgical season _____

Date_____ Day_____ Time_____

Gathering Procession: ☐ Yes ☐ No

   Origin of procession _____

   Route of procession_____

*Song of Gathering _____

Penitential Rite _____

Glory to God _____

Responsorial Psalm _____

*Gospel Acclamation _____

General Intercessions_____

Procession with the Gifts ☐ Yes ☐ No

   Music _____

Eucharistic Prayer _____

*Holy, Holy_____

*Eucharistic Acclamation_____

*Other Acclamations (for use with Eucharistic Prayers for Masses with
         Children)

*Great Amen _____

Lord's Prayer and Doxology _____

Lamb of God _____

*Communion Song_____

Recessional Song _____

*These moments are to be your first musical priorities in the liturgy. They call
for singing *by the entire assembly* before any other musical moments are added.

3. The Liturgy of the Hours_____

Suggested Morning and Evening Prayer Formats for Daytime and Evening Classroom Use

The Liturgy of the Hours is the second of the two official liturgies of the Church (the first being the Eucharistic liturgy, within which many of the sacraments take place). The purpose of the Liturgy of the Hours is to maintain the spirit of the Eucharist throughout the moments, hours, and days of the week. We mark the hours of each day in prayer so that we will remember God in all that we think and do.

As is true for the Eucharistic liturgy, our felt experience of prayer in this format can be greatly influenced by how the ritual is "performed" by its participants. The format itself will not ensure prayer. All of the concerns expressed in the introduction to this book, therefore, regarding the need for interior reflective preparation prior to prayer, also apply here.

For classroom use, we have outlined simplified forms of the traditional rituals for Morning and Evening Prayer. We hope that should you and your class undertake to join in this prayer of the universal Church, you will find it an inspiring and gratifying way in which to pray together.

MORNING PRAYER

This prayer form could be used to begin regular or religious education classes in the morning. Students could take turns acting as prayer leader.

Focus of Morning Prayer. Praise of our Creator and thanksgiving for creation. Individual and communal consecration of the day to God.

Main Character of Morning Prayer. Songs of praise, usually using psalm texts.

Symbolic Action at Morning Prayer. We bless ourselves as a remembrance of our baptism from a common bowl of holy water as we enter the prayer space, or we are sprinkled with holy water during the singing or speaking of the morning psalm. We touch or are touched by the water in order that we might keep in touch with the covenant relationship we entered with our God through the waters of our baptism.

1. Invitatory

This is an invitation to pray, not just as individuals but as a community. It can be either spoken or sung, and it calls the people who are gathered out of quiet, individual prayer into active, communal prayer. Each prayer time throughout the Liturgy of the Hours begins with quiet time and moves into song. The traditional text of the morning invitatory is as follows:

> **Leader:** Lord, open our lips,
> **Response:** And we shall proclaim your praise.
> **Leader:** Glory to God in the highest,
> **Response:** And peace to God's people on earth.

2. Morning Song

The character of this song is to be that of full, joyous praise of God in thanksgiving for creation. Choose a song that is energizing and which the students sing enthusiastically.

3. Morning Psalm

The traditional morning psalm is Psalm 63. This or another psalm of praise could be read responsorially, with one student reading the verses or several students each reading a verse. The ideal would be to sing this psalm. The response to Psalm 63 is "In the shadow of your wings I sing for joy." A musical setting of this refrain could be used as the morning song on occasion, or regularly with primary grade students. A full psalm setting could also be used as the morning song. In either of these ways, the morning song and psalm can be combined into one sung moment, simplifying the format even further.

4. Psalm Prayer

The student leader could be asked in advance to write a prayer of praise using an image from the morning psalm, or else he or she could be asked to pray spontaneously on the themes of thanksgiving for creation and/or of consecration of the day to God.

5. Reading

One or two sentences from one of the readings of the day could be proclaimed by one of the students, or successive brief excerpts from the coming Sunday readings could be proclaimed each morning. Morning prayer is not a Liturgy of the Word, so whatever reading is chosen should always be brief.

6. Silent Time

Ideally, time for silent reflection should follow the reading.

7. General Intercessions

Two or three brief prayers could be written by one of the students, perhaps using the same set of prayers each day for a given week. Or this time could be devoted to spontaneous prayer, allowing anyone present to join in. The character of these prayers should continue to focus on praise for creation, consecrating the day to God, and remembering God in all that we do.

8. The Lord's Prayer

The general intercessions culminate with the communal praying of the Lord's Prayer. You might wish to include the doxology with this prayer ("For the kingdom . . ."), since it consecrates all of creation to God, much in keeping with the entire focus of Morning Prayer.

9. Blessing

The student leader offers the blessing. To bless one another simply means to ask for God's remembrance, love, and fullness of life on behalf of one another. In the leadership of this spoken prayer and bodily gesture (hands raised over the heads of all present, palms down), students have an opportunity to experience a deeper involvement and participation in their prayer with others.

10. Sign of Peace

Morning Prayer concludes with offering one another a sign of the peaceful presence of Christ in our hearts. The sign of peace is meant to be a bodily prayer gesture that shows our commitment to be like Christ in all that we do. With this outward sign we pray that we will be strengthened in our efforts to move beyond the barriers that keep us from fully loving one another.

EVENING PRAYER

This prayer form could be used to begin evening religious education classes or high school evening retreats. Students could take turns acting as prayer leader.

Begin in darkness.

Focus of Evening Prayer. Jesus Christ is the light that shines in the darkness. Thanksgiving for the gifts of the closing day. Seeking protection from evil forces. Forgiveness for those times during the day when we have not allowed the fullness of God's love to guide our thoughts and actions.

Main Character of Evening Prayer. Songs of praise, thanksgiving, and surrender to the light of Christ, usually using psalm texts.

Symbolic Action at Evening Prayer. We begin in darkness and light a candle in recognition of Christ's powerful presence among us. At the same time, we burn incense as we lift our pleading hearts to God. (A few pieces of incense placed on a single lighted charcoal in an open bowl of sand, gravel, or cat litter provides sufficient incense for a brief prayer time.)

1. *Invitatory*

This is an invitation to pray, not just as individuals but as a community. It can be either spoken or sung, and it calls the people who are gathered out of quiet, individual prayer into active, communal prayer. Each prayer time throughout the Liturgy of the Hours begins with quiet time and moves into song. The traditional text of the evening invitatory is as follows:

> **Leader:** Jesus Christ is the light of the world.
> **Response:** A light no darkness can extinguish.
>
> *or*
>
> **Leader:** Light and peace in Jesus Christ our Lord.
> **Response:** Thanks be to God.

2. *Evening Song*

The character of this song is to be that of rejoicing in Jesus Christ as the light of the world. Choose a song that is energizing and which the students sing enthusiastically.

3. *Evening Psalm*

The traditional evening psalm is Psalm 141. This or another psalm that pleads for God's assistance and protection could be read responsorially, with one student reading the verses or several students each reading a verse. The ideal would be to sing this psalm. The response to Psalm 141 is "My prayers rise like incense, my hands like an evening offering." A musical setting of this refrain could be used as the evening song on occasion, or regularly with primary grade students. A full psalm setting could also be used as the evening song. In either of these ways, the evening song and psalm can be combined into one sung moment, simplifying the format even further.

4. *Psalm Prayer*

The student leader could be asked in advance to write a prayer using an image from the evening psalm, or else he or she could be asked to pray spontaneously on the themes of praise, thanksgiving, and/or forgiveness.

5. *Reading*

One or two sentences from one of the readings of the day could be proclaimed by one of the students, or a brief excerpt from the coming Sunday readings could be proclaimed. Evening Prayer is not a Liturgy of the Word, so whatever reading is chosen should always be brief.

6. *Silent Time*

Ideally, time for silent reflection should follow the reading.

7. *General Intercessions*

Two or three brief prayers could be written by one of the students. Or this time could be devoted to spontaneous prayer, allowing anyone present to join in. The character of these prayers should continue to focus on praise, thanksgiving, and forgiveness.

8. *The Lord's Prayer*

The general intercessions culminate with the communal praying of the Lord's Prayer. You might wish to include the doxology with this prayer (''For the kingdom . . .''), since it reaffirms our recognition that all of creation rests in God's hands, much in keeping with the entire focus of Evening Prayer.

9. *Blessing*

The student leader offers the blessing. To bless one another simply means to ask for God's remembrance, love, and fullness of life on behalf of one another. In the leadership of this spoken prayer and bodily gesture (hands raised over the heads of all present, palms down), students have an opportunity to experience a deeper involvement and participation in their prayer with others.

10. Sign of Peace

Evening Prayer concludes with offering one another a sign of the peaceful presence of Christ in our hearts. The sign of peace is meant to be a bodily prayer gesture that shows our commitment to be like Christ in all that we do. With this outward sign we pray that we will be strengthened in our efforts to move beyond the barriers that keep us from fully loving one another.

Morning Prayer

Environment:
- ☐ Classroom, at desks
- ☐ Classroom, in a circle
- ☐ Church
- ☐ School grounds outdoors
- ☐ School multipurpose room
- ☐ Other _____

Posture: Morning Prayer is usually prayed standing (except, perhaps, during the reading and the silent time that follows it).

Leader: *(leads the invitatory, psalm prayer, Lord's Prayer, blessing, and sign of peace)*

_____

Song Leader: *(leads the morning song; also leads the response to the psalm and the Lord's Prayer, if these are sung)*

_____

Invitatory:
> **Leader:** Lord, open our lips,
> **Response:** And we shall proclaim your praise.
> **Leader:** Glory to God in the highest,
> **Response:** And peace to God's people on earth.

*Morning Song*_____

   Song book_____   Page_____   Number_____

Morning Psalm Number_____

   Song book_____   Page_____   Number_____

Response: _____

Psalm verses handled by: ☐ Cantor(s)   ☐ Reader(s)

1._____   3._____

2._____   4._____

Psalm Prayer

*Reading:*_____ Assembly will: ☐ Stand   ☐ Sit

   Proclaimed by _____

Silent Time

General Intercessions

   Response: _____

   Written and read by _____

The Lord's Prayer ☐ Sung   ☐ Spoken

   With doxology?   ☐ Yes   ☐ No

Blessing Text_____

_____

_____ **Response:** Amen.

   Written by _____

Sign of Peace Invitational text _____

_____

   Written by _____

Evening Prayer

Environment:

   ☐ Classroom, at desks   ☐ School grounds outdoors

   ☐ Classroom, in a circle   ☐ School multipurpose room

   ☐ Church   ☐ Other _____

Posture: Evening Prayer is usually prayed standing (except, perhaps, during the reading and the silent time that follows it).

Leader: *(leads the invitatory, psalm prayer, Lord's Prayer, blessing, and sign of peace)*

_____

Song Leader: *(leads the evening song; also leads the response to the psalm and the Lord's Prayer, if these are sung)*

_____

Invitatory
> **Leader:** Jesus Christ is the light of the world.
> **Response:** A light no darkness can extinguish.
> > *or*
> **Leader:** Light and peace in Jesus Christ our Lord.
> **Response:** Thanks be to God.

Evening Song _____
> Song book_____ Page_____ Number_____

Evening Psalm Number _____
> Song book_____ Page_____ Number_____
> **Response** _____
> Psalm verses handled by: ☐ Cantor(s) ☐ Reader(s)
> 1._____ 3._____
> 2._____ 4._____

Psalm Prayer

*Reading*_____ Assembly will: ☐ Stand ☐ Sit
> Proclaimed by _____

Silent Time

General Intercessions
> *Response:* _____
> Written and read by _____

The Lord's Prayer ☐ Sung ☐ Spoken
> With doxology? ☐ Yes ☐ No

Blessing: Text _____

_____

_____ **Response:** Amen.

Written by _____

Sign of Peace Invitational text _____

_____

Written by _____

Appendix————————————————

STUDENT LITURGY COMMITTEES

How we understand Church shapes how we pray at liturgy. If we understand ourselves each to be integral members of the Church, and if we feel drawn to take an active part in the life of the Church, then we will be more likely to participate fully, consciously, and actively in liturgical prayer.

We, therefore, highly recommend each school seriously consider establishing a student liturgy committee. A biyearly overlapping membership on the committee would help establish a sense of continuity from year to year. The committee would be made up predominantly of students.

The group could be led by a member of the faculty, who would be supported by the school in pursuing continuing educational opportunities in liturgy. The role of this advisor would resemble that of a student-council advisor, only here it would call for the development of skills in liturgy preparation and formation.

BEYOND THIS BOOKLET

Even as we look forward to the fullness of God's reign, "we live and move and have our being" in God's love among us here and now. In every liturgy it is this very dwelling of God among us that we celebrate. We would like to thank you for caring enough about the dynamics of celebrating good liturgy to have read this far! We heartily wish to encourage you in your endeavors to help students prepare carefully for liturgy.

Well-prepared liturgy can be a source of great hope and joy for all of us. In helping students prepare for it we manifest our care for them. For in the very process of preparing for liturgy we are drawn into closer union with one another and with our God. And our school liturgies become the work—and the prayer—of students and teachers alike.

THE LITURGY DOCUMENTS

Appendix to the General Instruction for Dioceses of the United States (1969)

The Appendix to the General Instruction, found in the Sacramentary, gives specific instructions regarding cultural adaptations of the liturgy for the Church in the United States.

Constitution on the Sacred Liturgy (1963)

This is the original Vatican II document on liturgy. It serves as an introduction to the process of reform and renewal called for by the council. It has pointed the way for liturgical studies in our time, many fruits of which are reflected in the postconciliar documents on liturgy.

Directory for Masses with Children (1973)

This document starts with the recognition that children pray differently than adults do. It clearly outlines which areas of the Catholic worship ritual can be tailored to the experience of children, while still preserving the richness of Church tradition and teaching.

Environment and Art in Catholic Worship (1978)

The final sentence of paragraph 4 of this document states: ''God does not need liturgy; people do, and people need their own art and styles of expression with which to celebrate.'' The document addresses some basic questions about art and styles of expression appropriate to worship. It provides a vision of liturgical prayer that is an inspiration not only for artists but for all who are involved in liturgical planning.

General Instruction on the Liturgy of the Hours (1971)

This document calls for, and outlines, the renewal of the prayer formerly known as the Divine Office, not only for priests and members of religious communities but for all members of the Catholic Church. The instruction explains the purpose of this communal prayer ritual, which has been a part of the Church's liturgical heritage for centuries, and details its format for the various hours of the day.

General Norms for the Liturgical Year (1969)

This document explains the Church system for ranking occasions for celebration, with Sunday being the primary feast. It also provides details on the celebration of the various seasons of the Church year.

General Instruction of the Roman Missal (1969)

The General Instruction is in the front pages of the Sacramentary. It provides basic information on the order of the Eucharistic liturgy and on the roles of the various liturgical ministries.

Lectionary for Mass: Introduction (1969, revised 1981)

This document introduces the reader to the Lectionary, which contains a three-year cycle of Sunday readings and a two-year cycle of weekday readings. It provides instruction on how we are to reverence and study the word of God and on how we are to proclaim this story of our salvation in public worship.

Liturgical Music Today (1982)

Liturgical Music Today is a supplement to Music in Catholic Worship. It addresses questions that arose in the ten-year interim between documents and also provides instruction on the use of music for other sacraments.

Music in Catholic Worship (1972)

Music in Catholic Worship establishes norms for evaluating the selection of music for Eucharistic liturgy and defines the function of music and the roles of musicians in the liturgy. It is an excellent resource for a simple study of Catholic worship ritual and theology.

Joan Patano Vos has served as a parish director of music, choir founder and director, and cantor. For three years she was the director of the office of worship for the diocese of Wichita. Joan is a liturgist at St. Paul the Apostle Church in New York City.

Timothy J. Vos has worked as a church musician and cantor in Toronto, Wichita, and New York City. He has written music for the liturgy, including his 1983 *Mass for Peace*, and is a musical playwright.